This Book Belongs To:

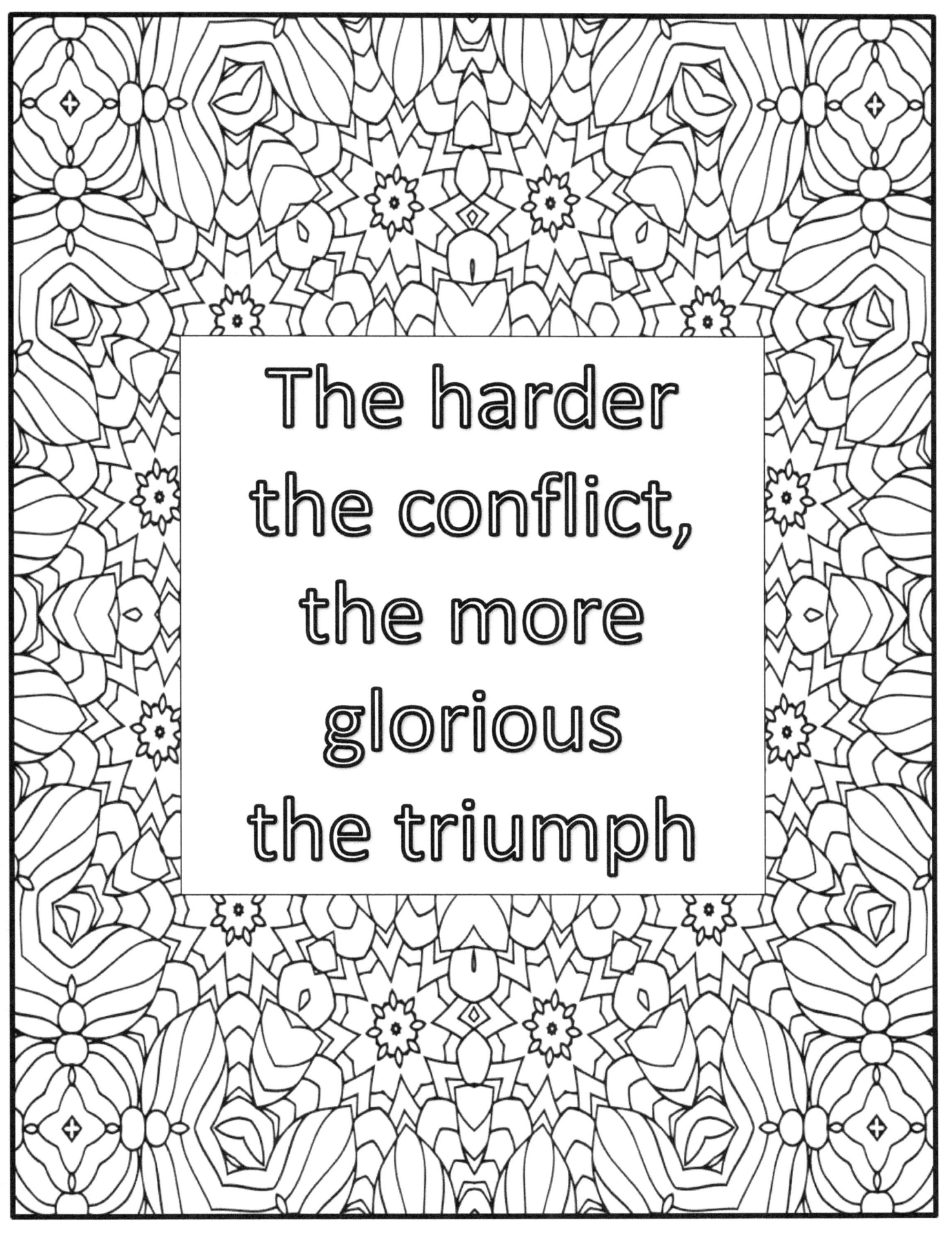

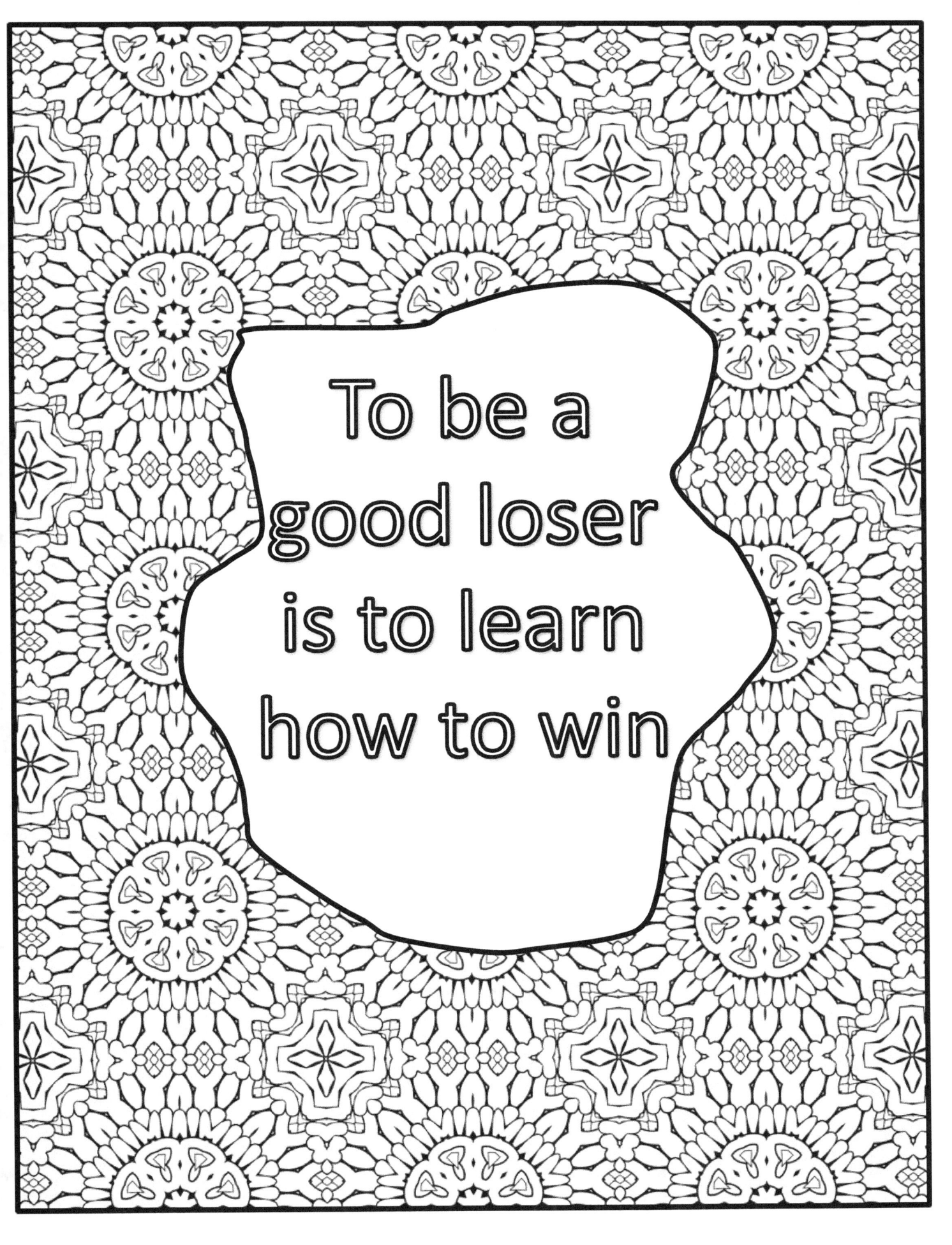

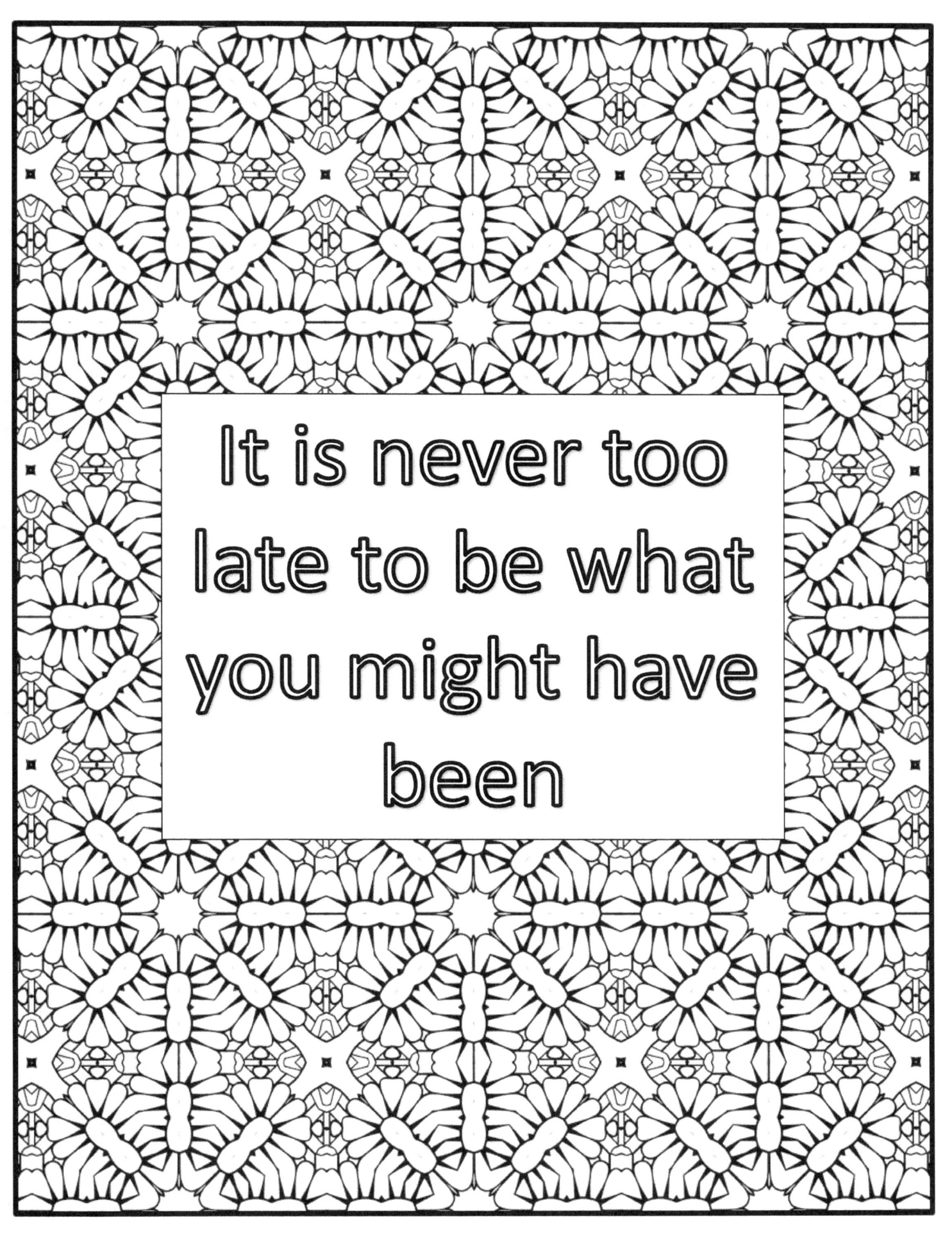

It is never too late to be what you might have been

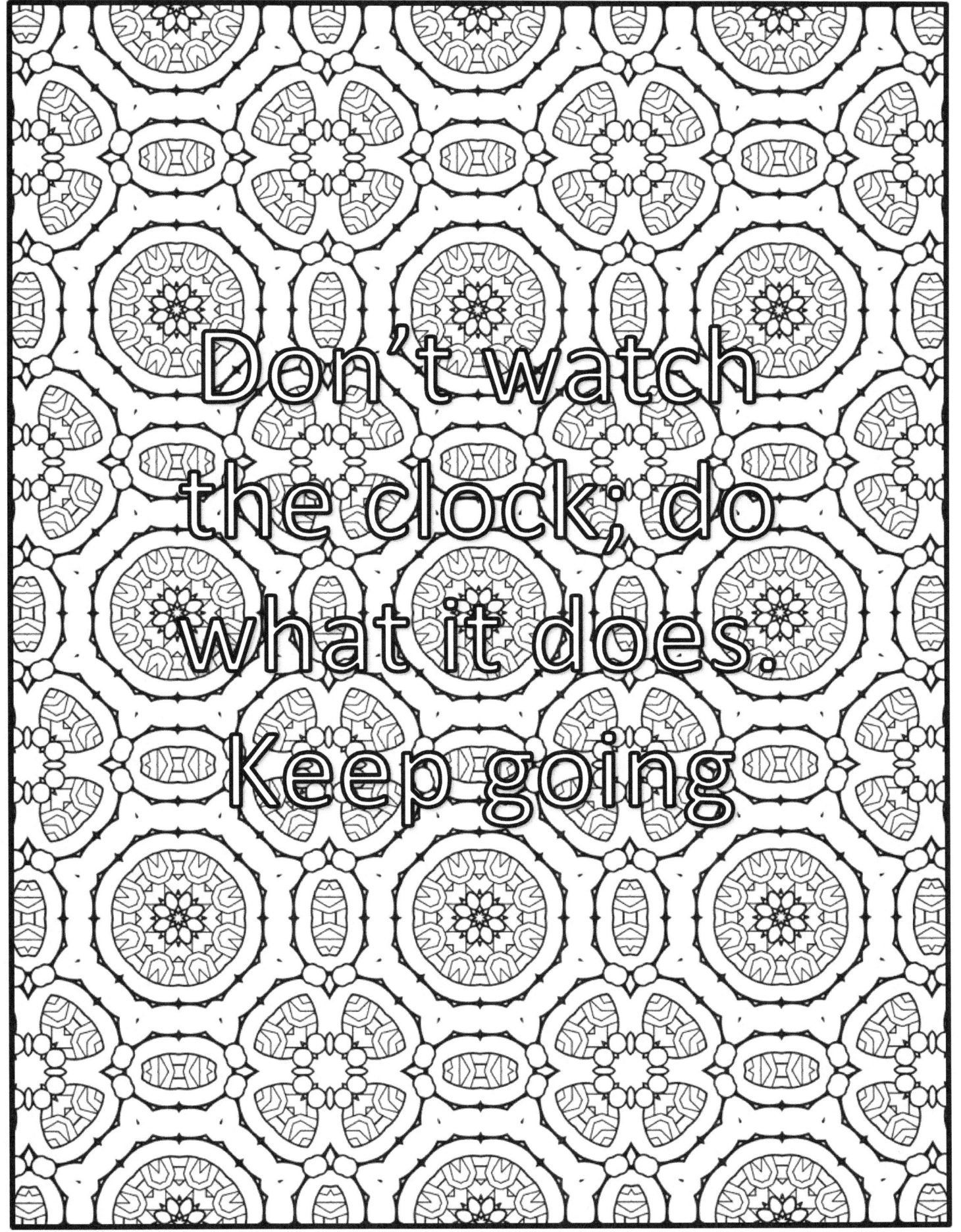

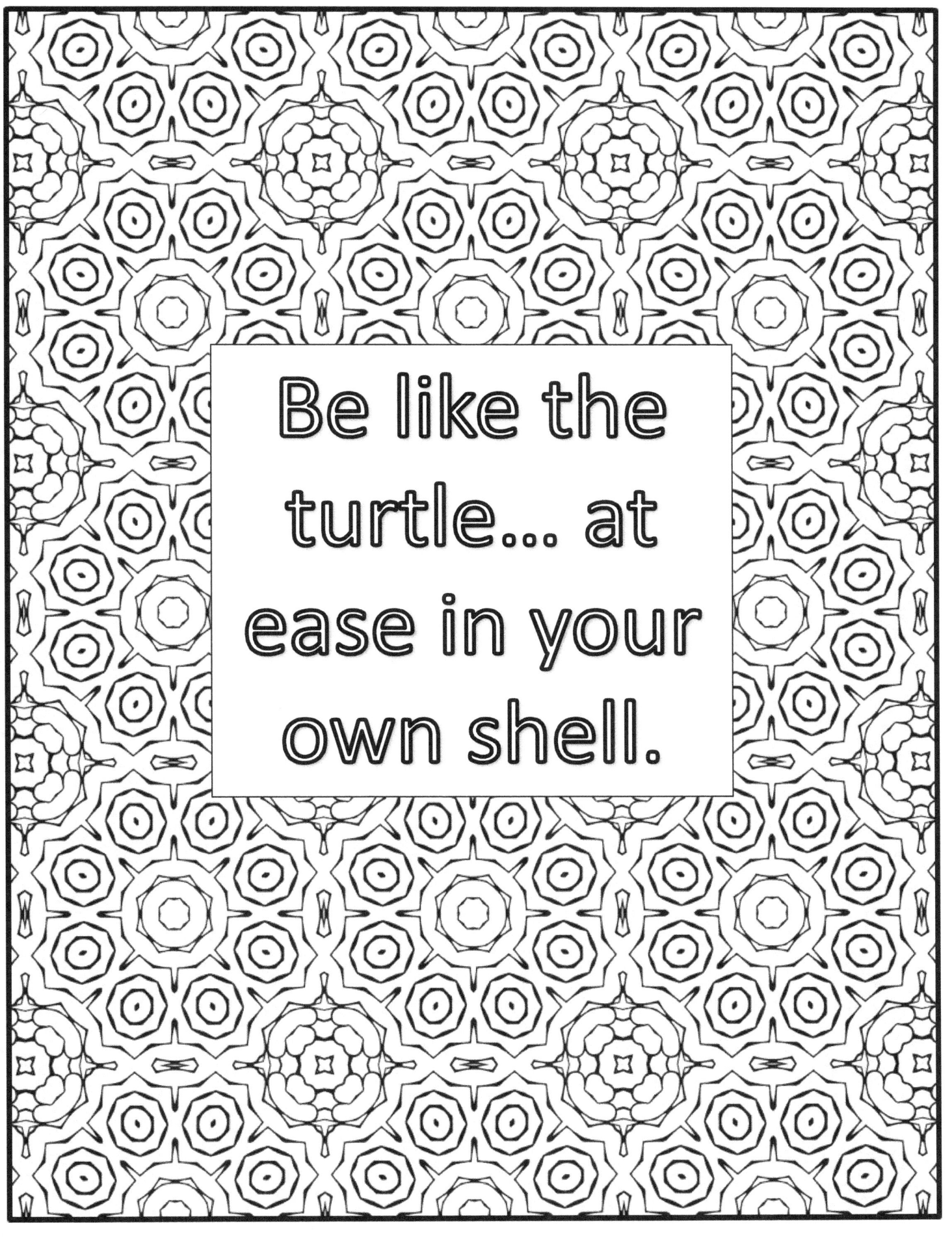

Be like the turtle... at ease in your own shell.

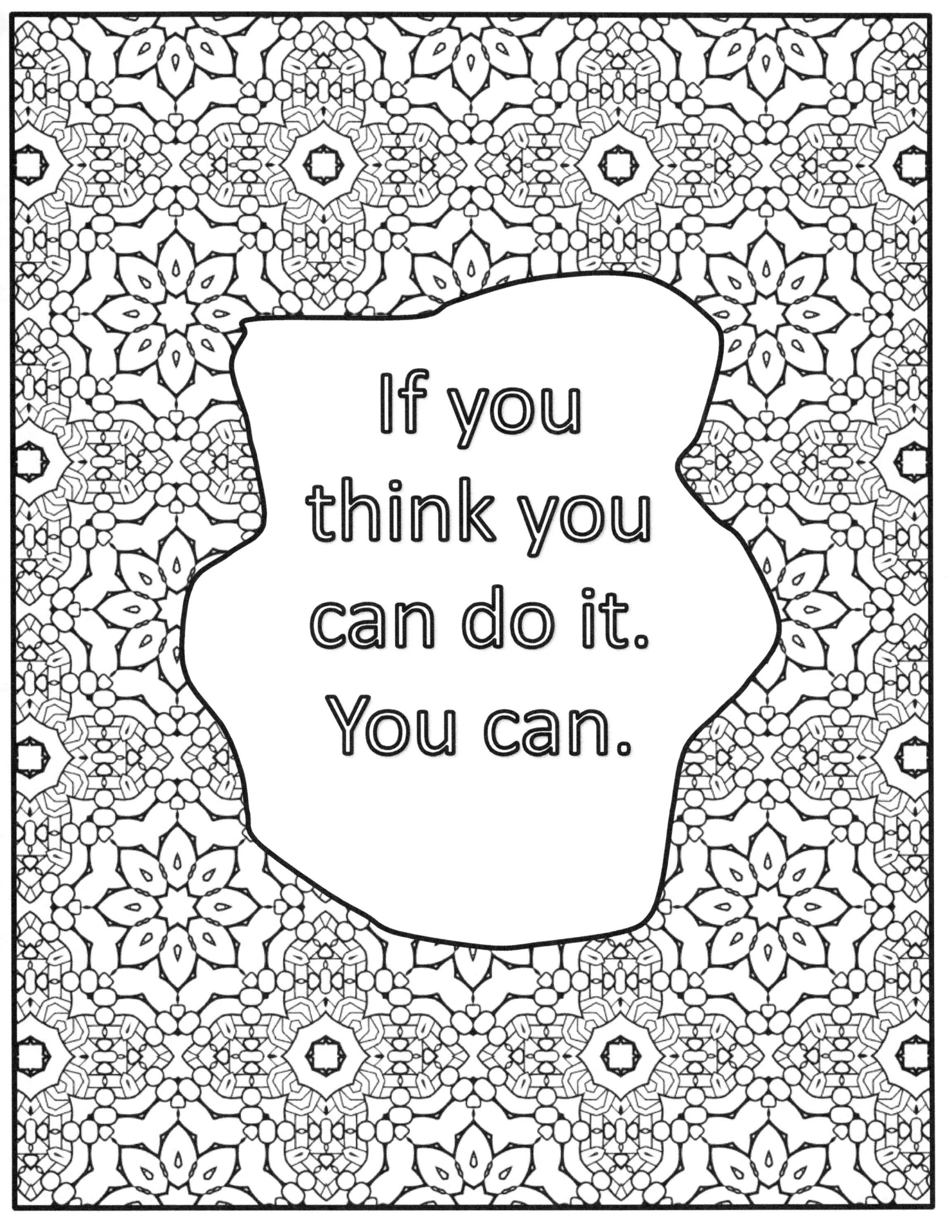

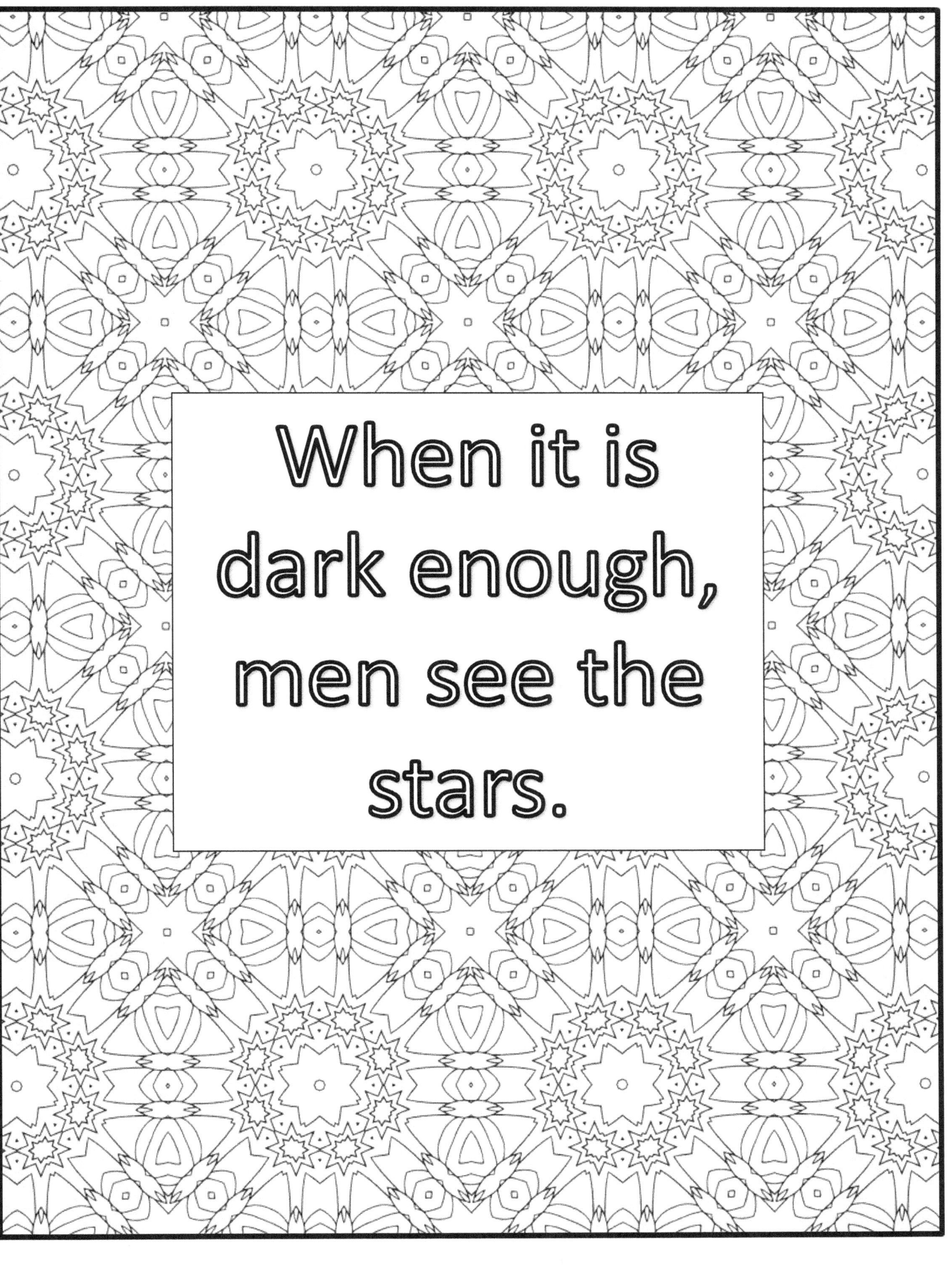

When it is dark enough, men see the stars.

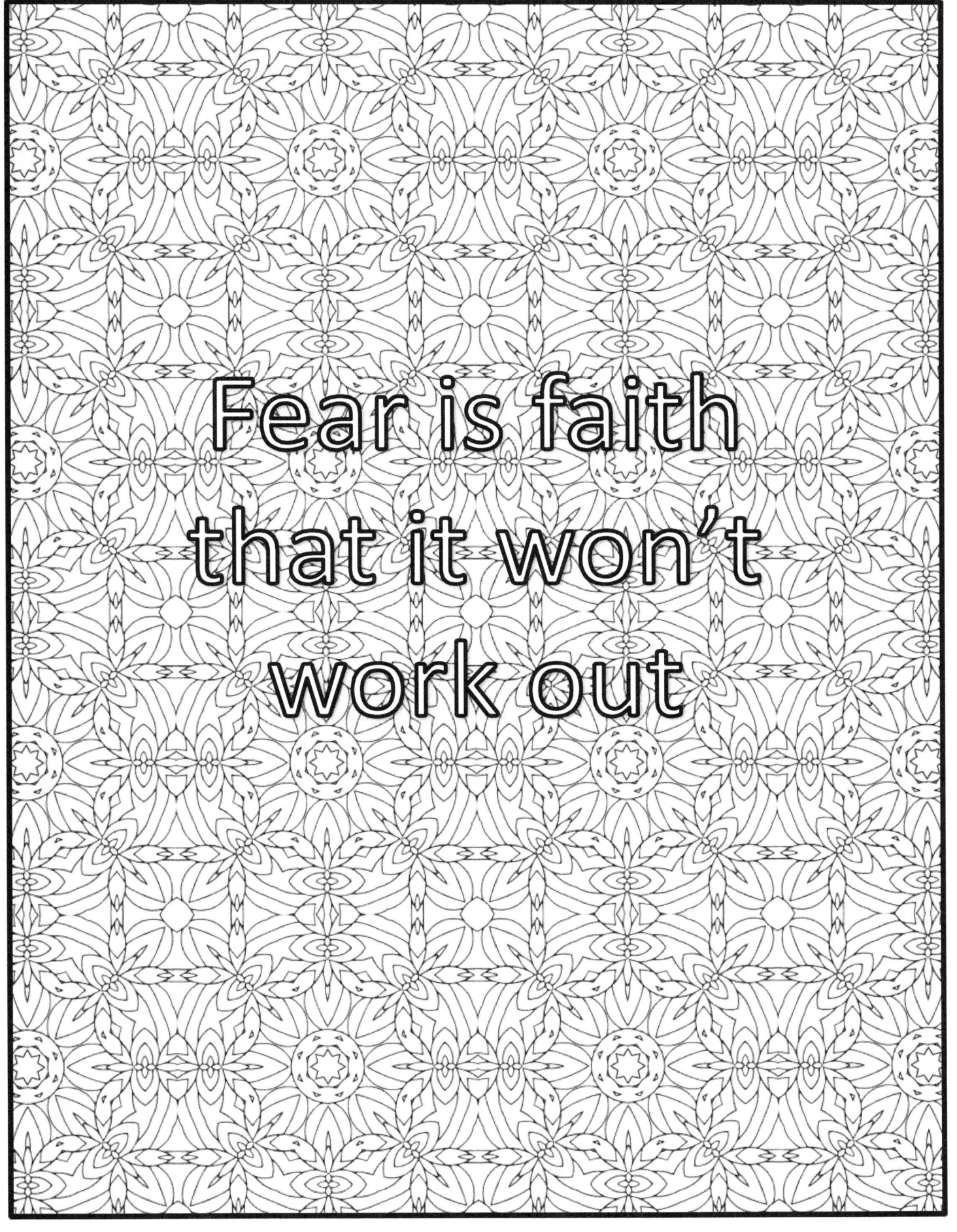

Fear is faith that it won't work out

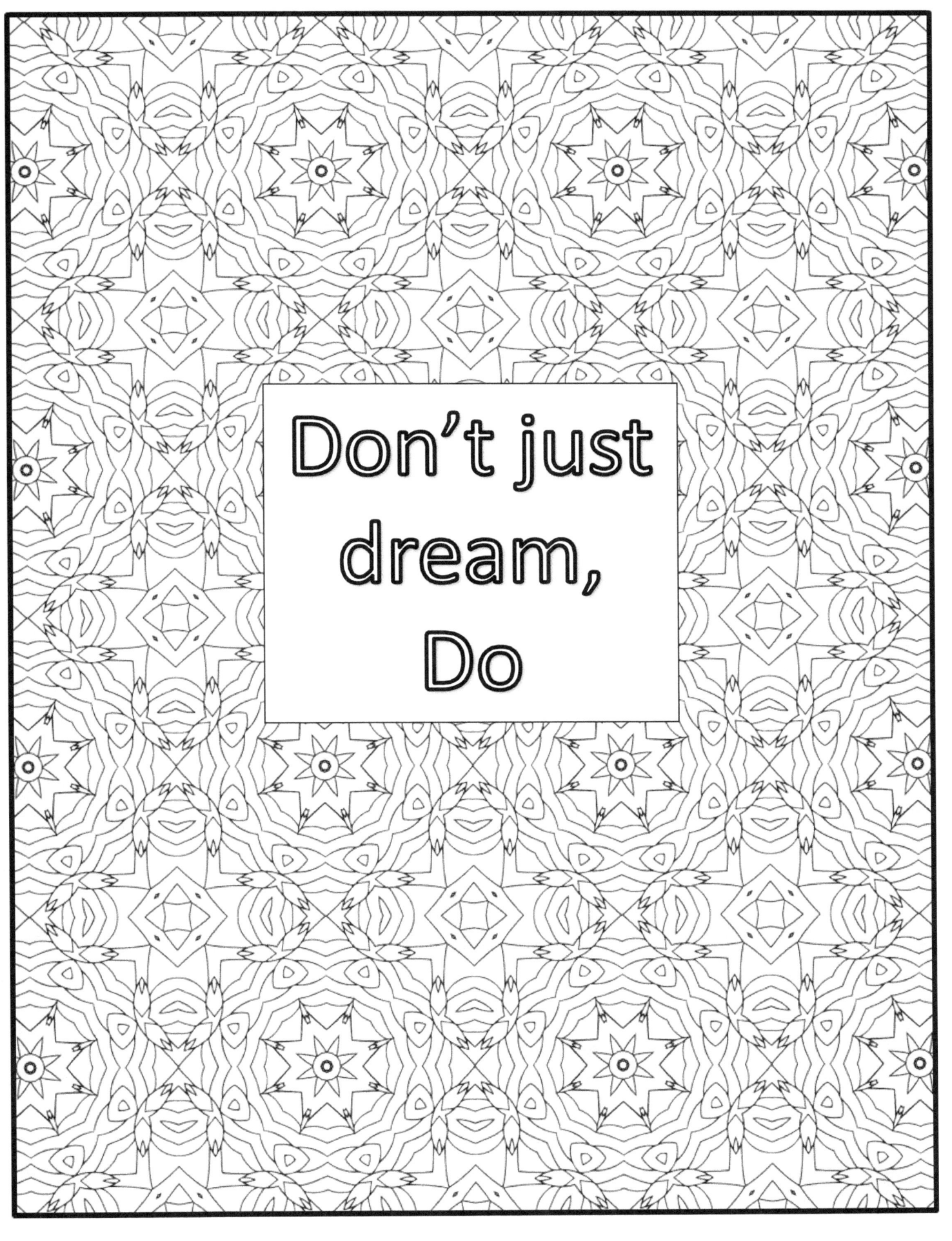

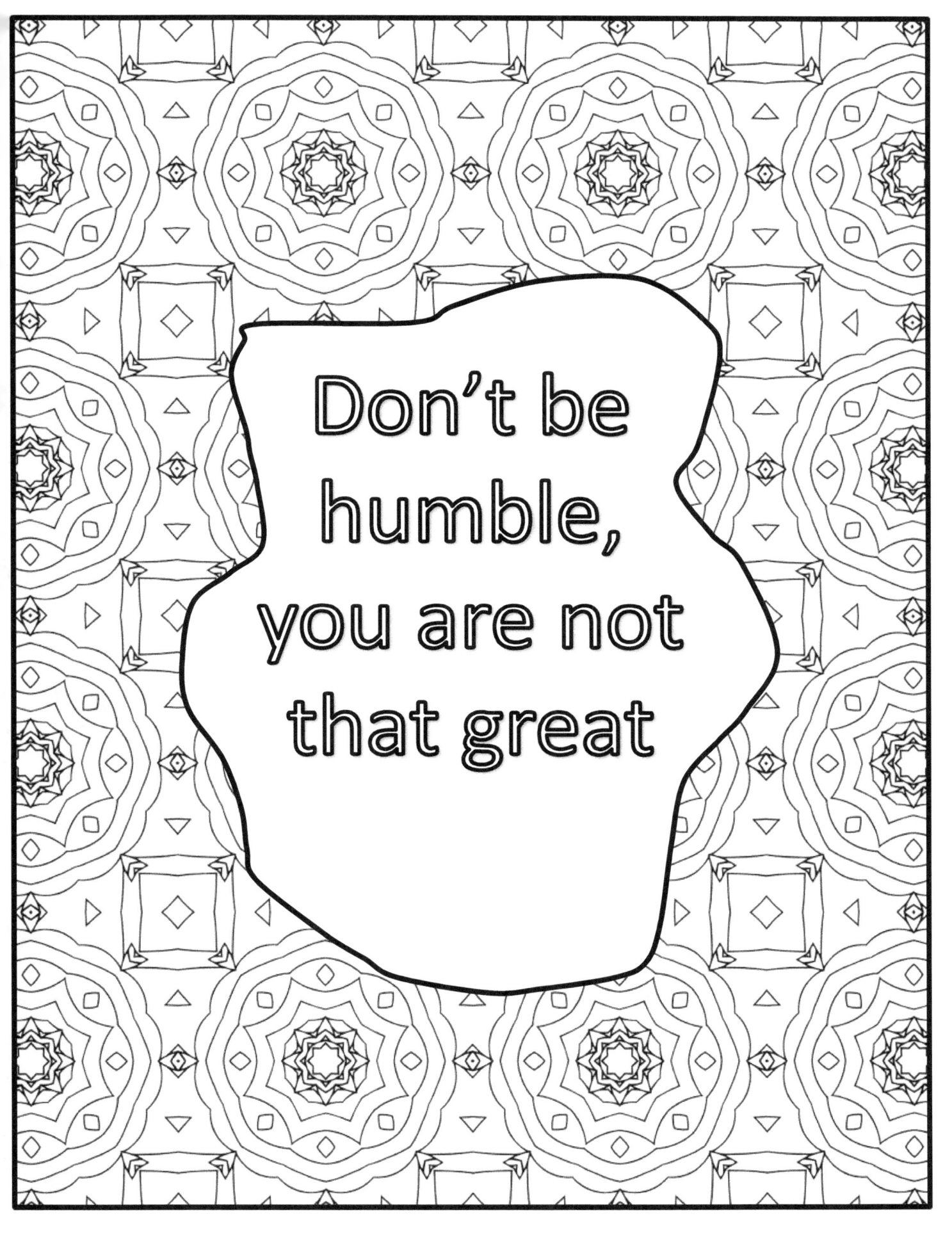

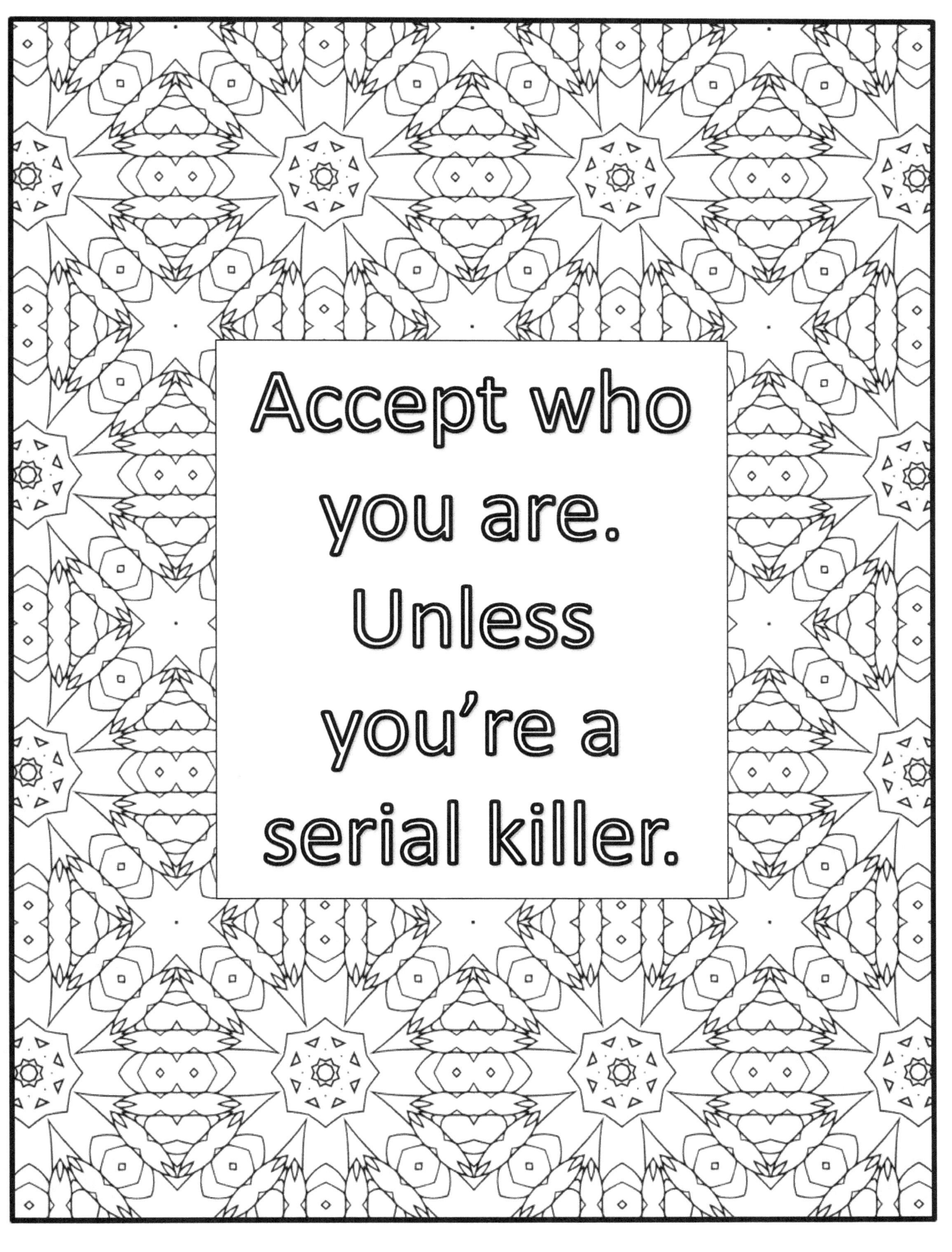

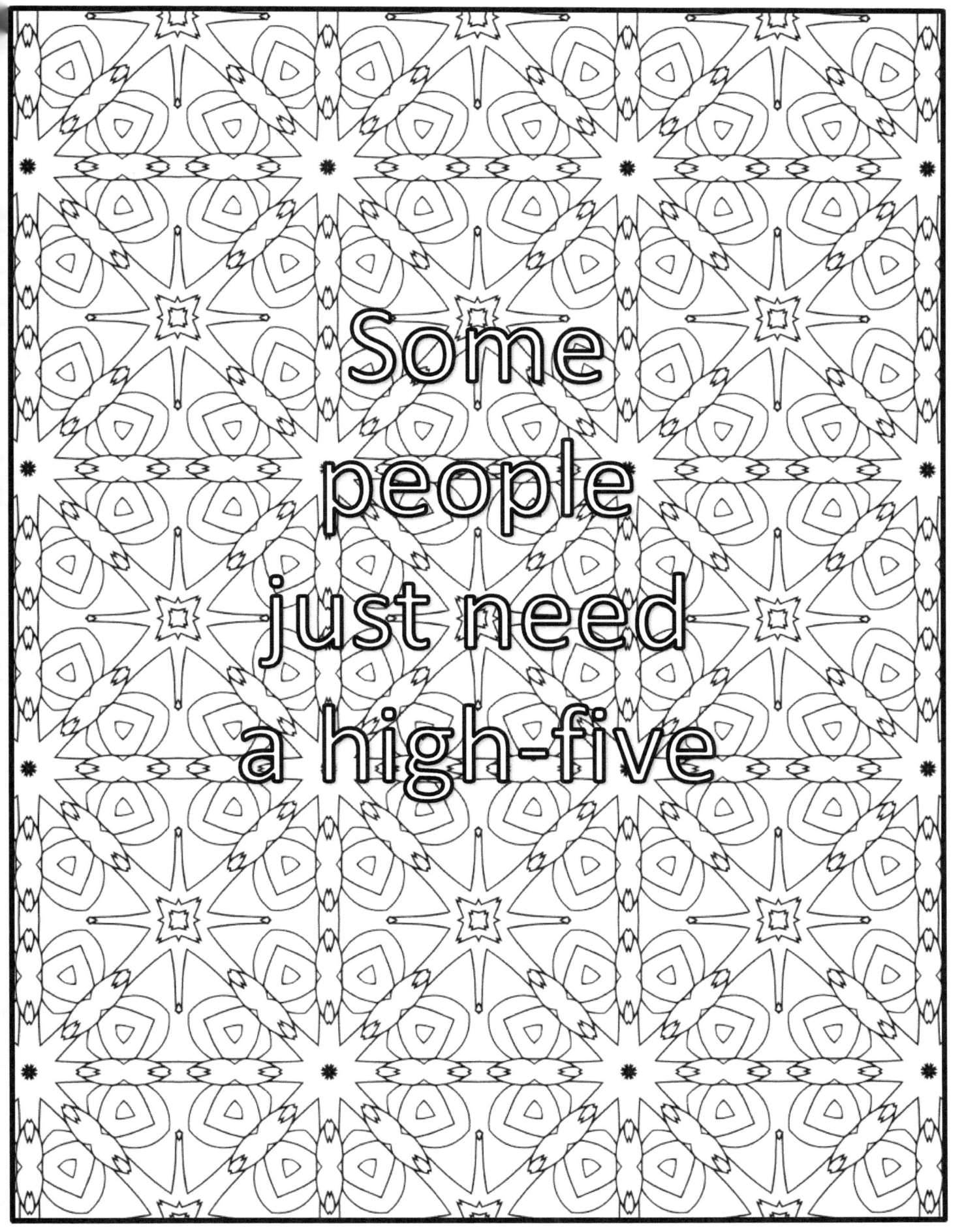

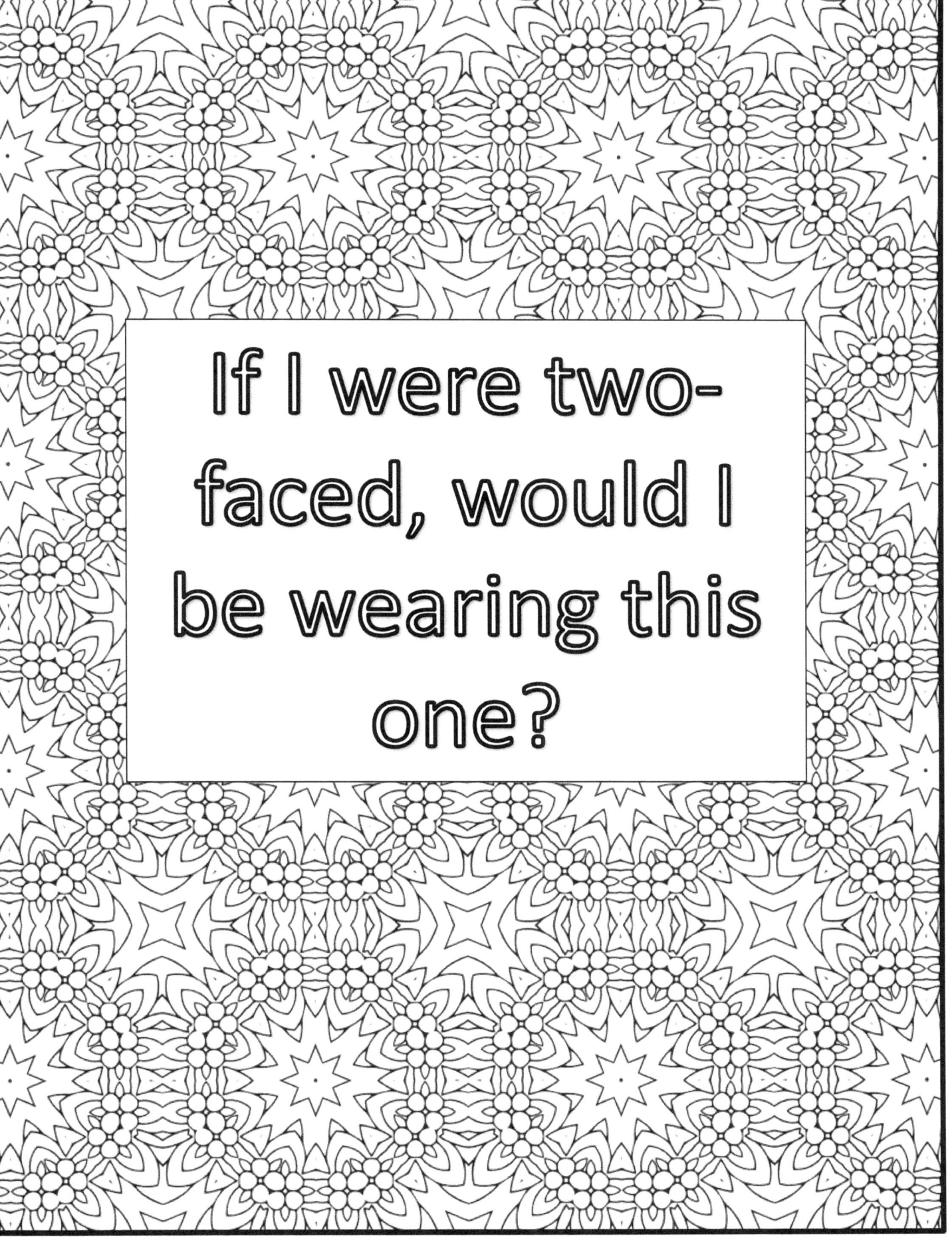

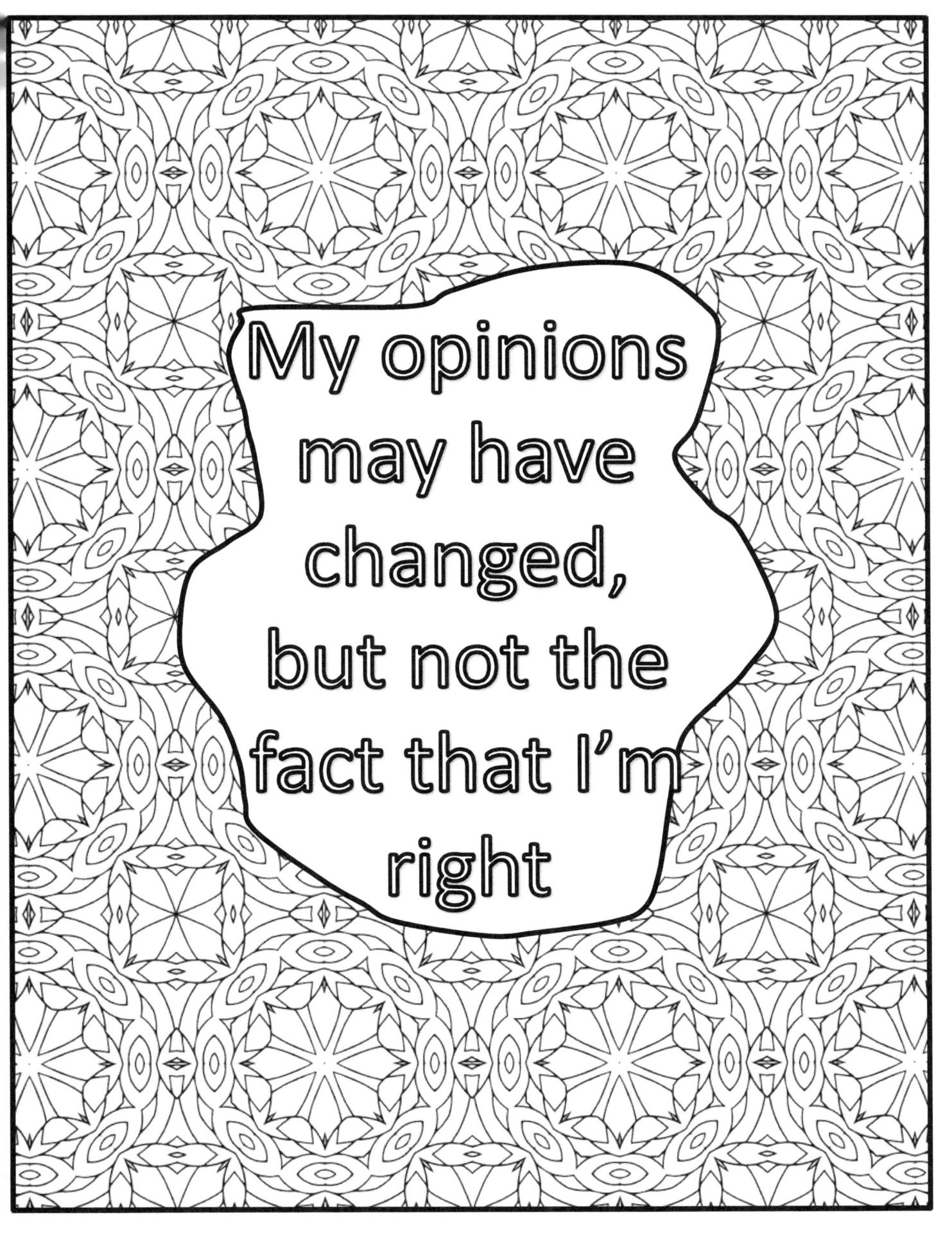

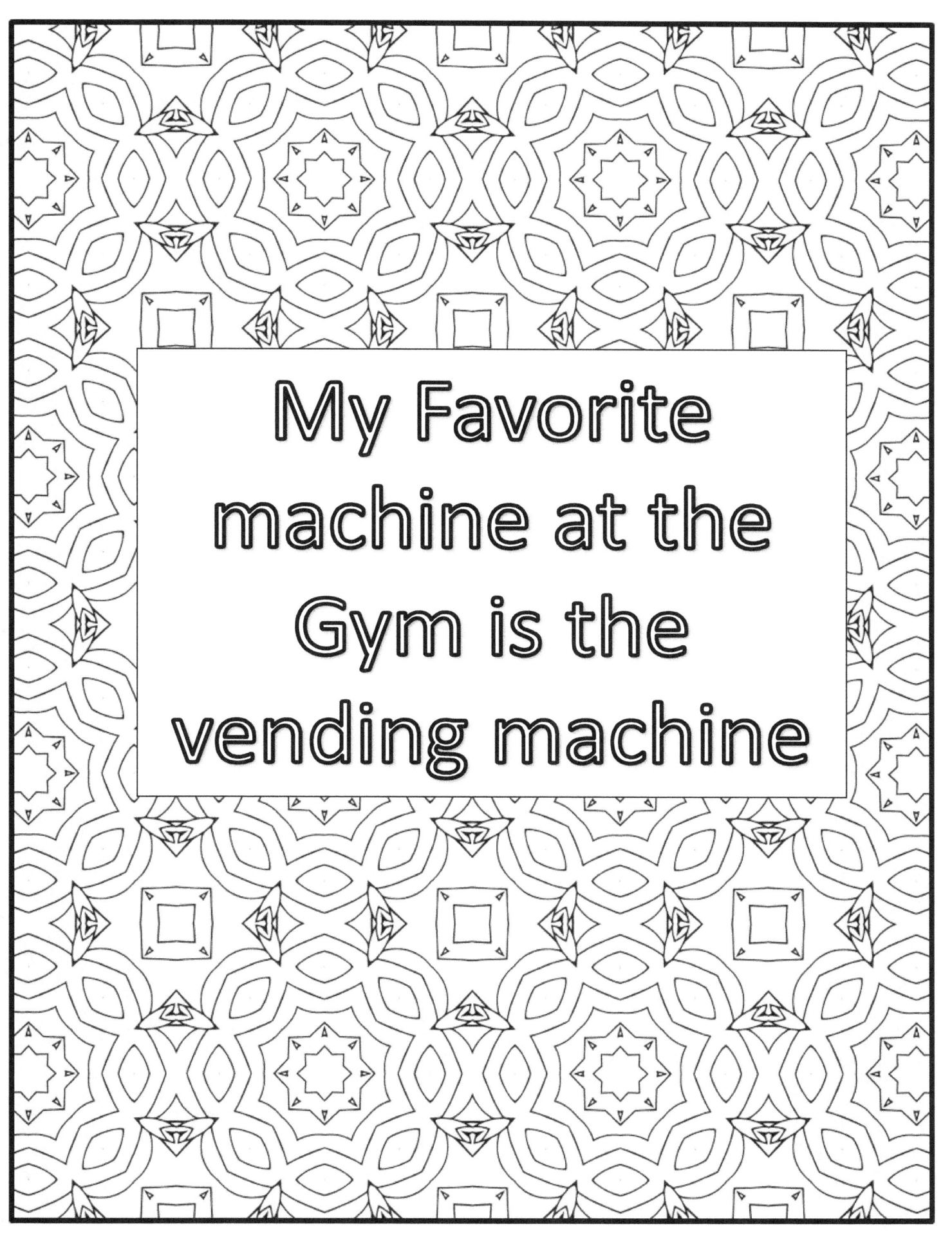

My Favorite machine at the Gym is the vending machine

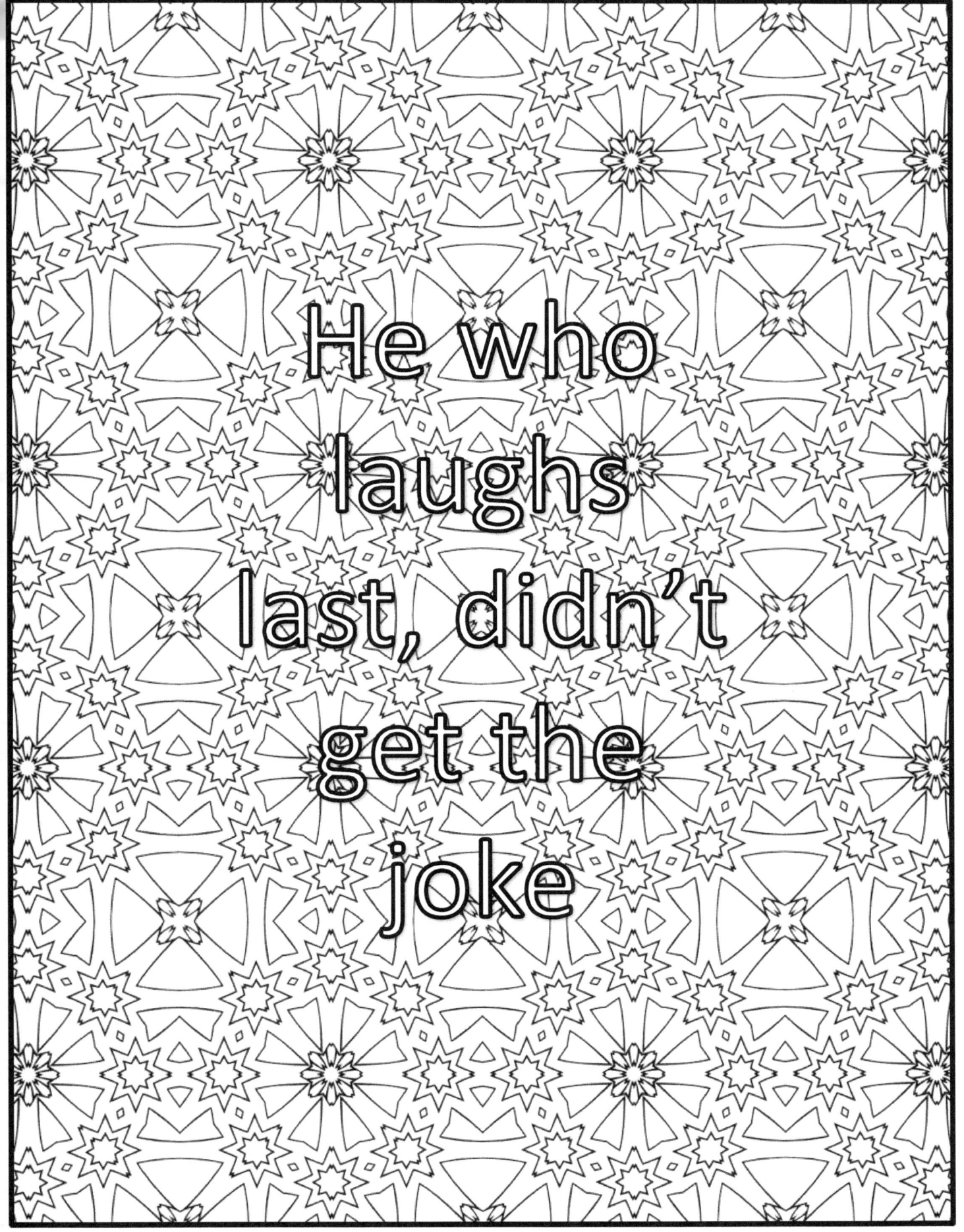

He who laughs last, didn't get the joke

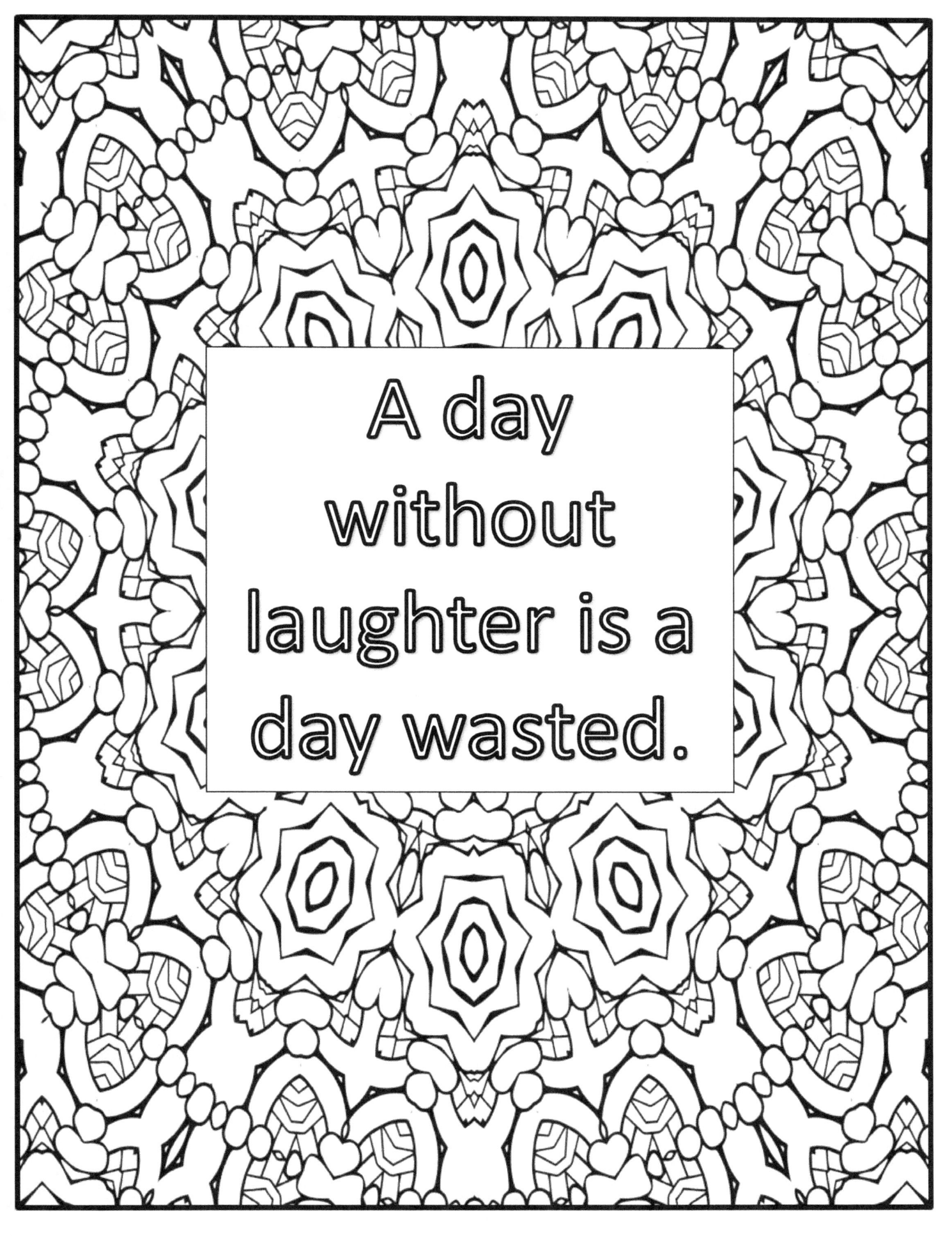

A day without laughter is a day wasted.

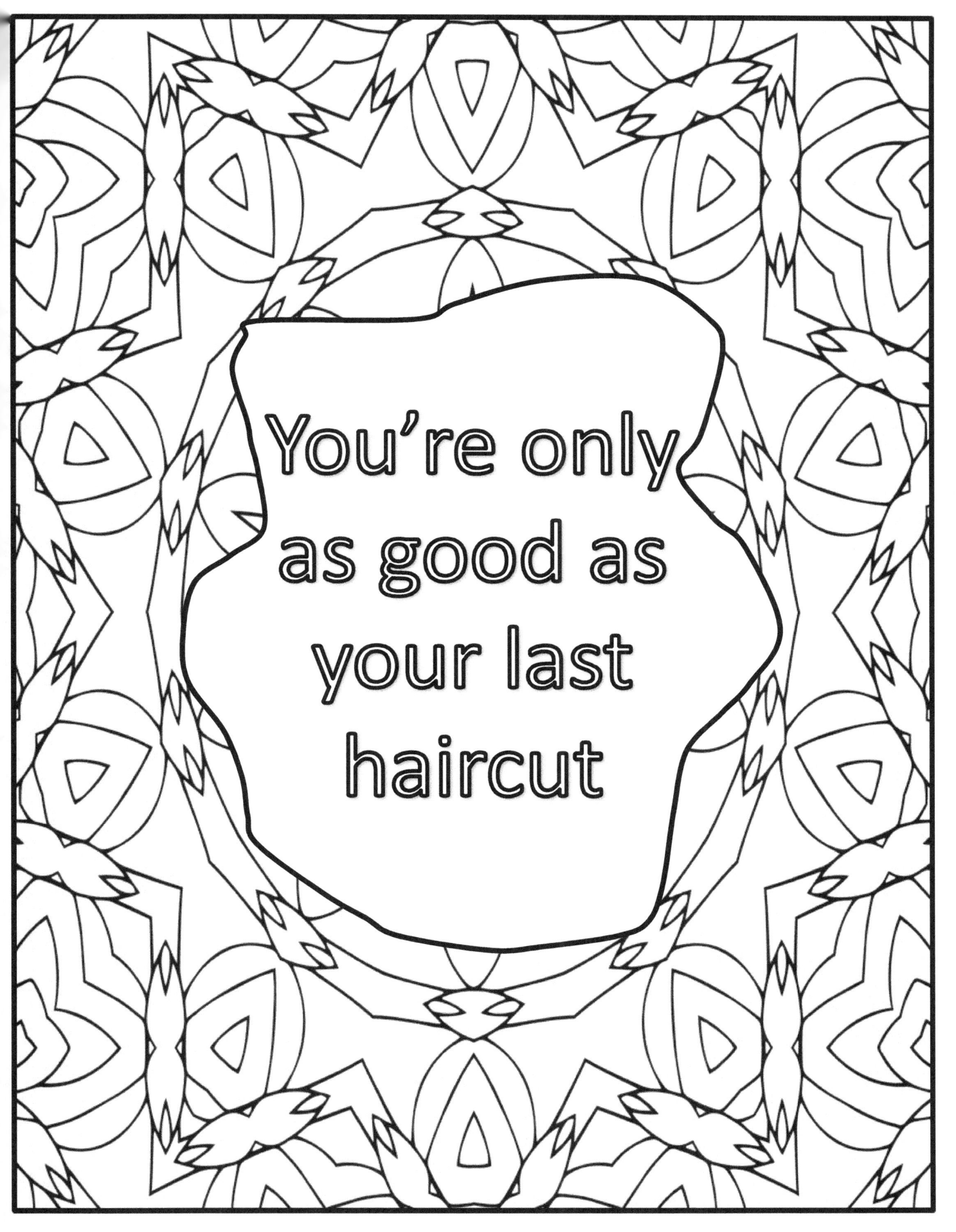

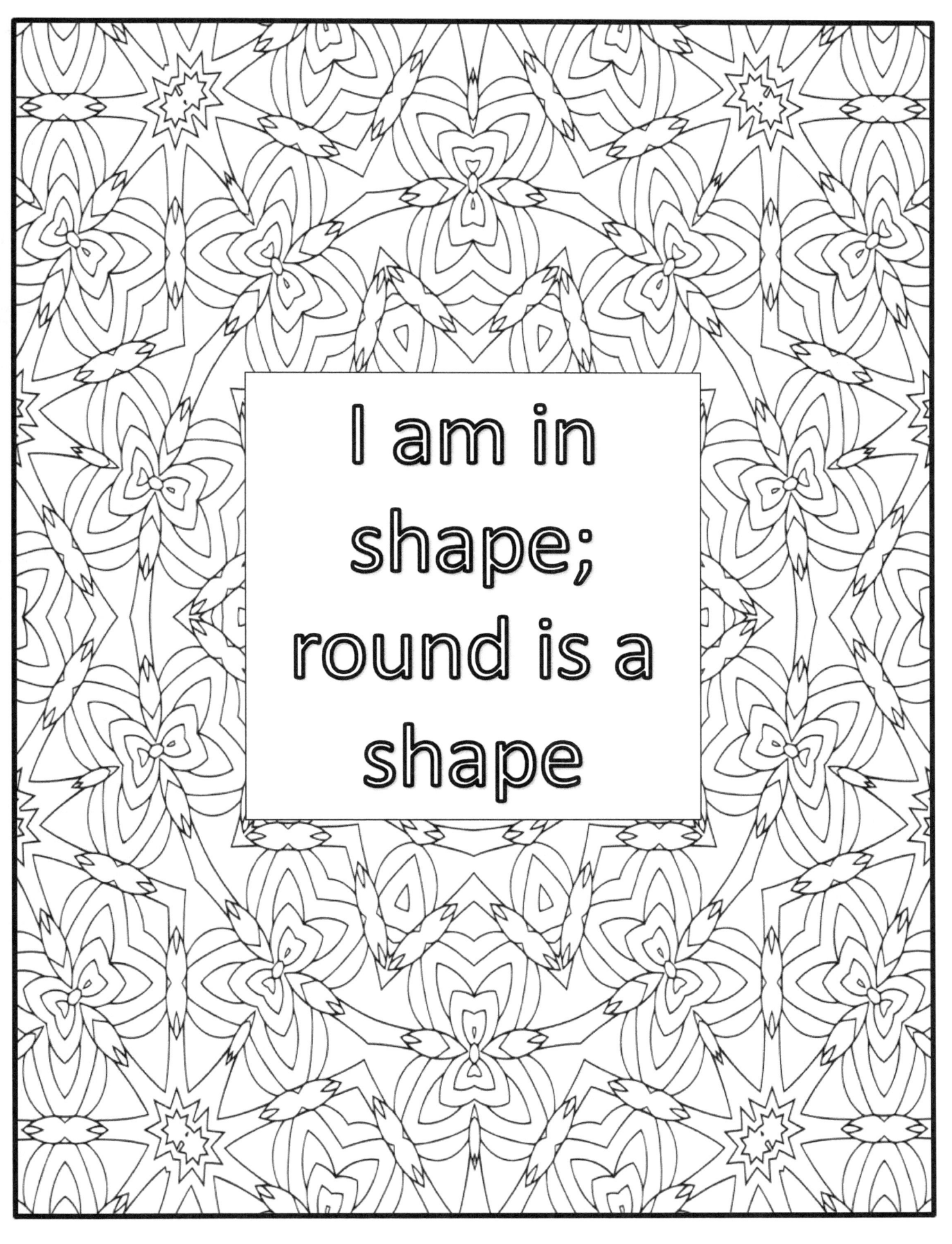

I am in shape; round is a shape

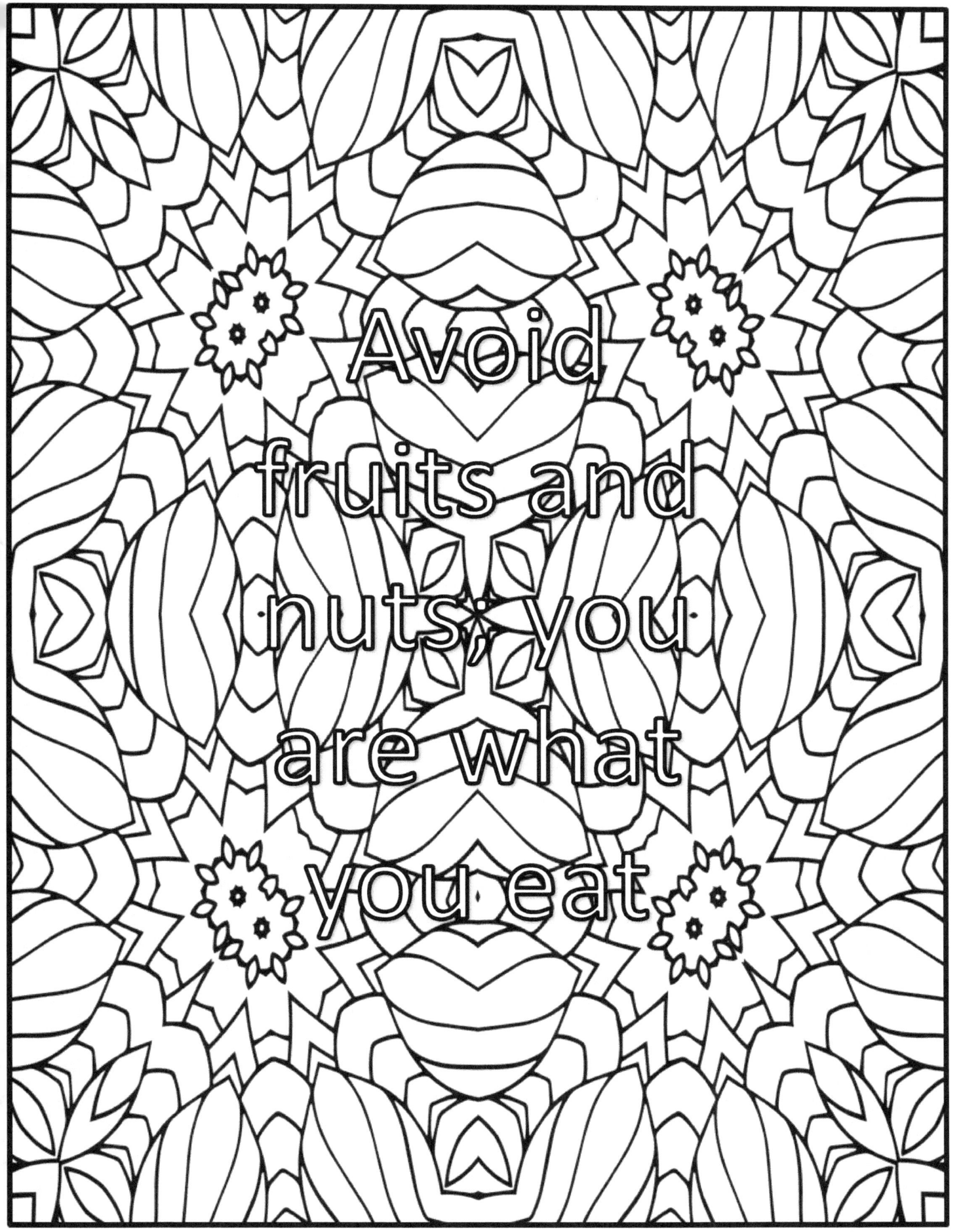

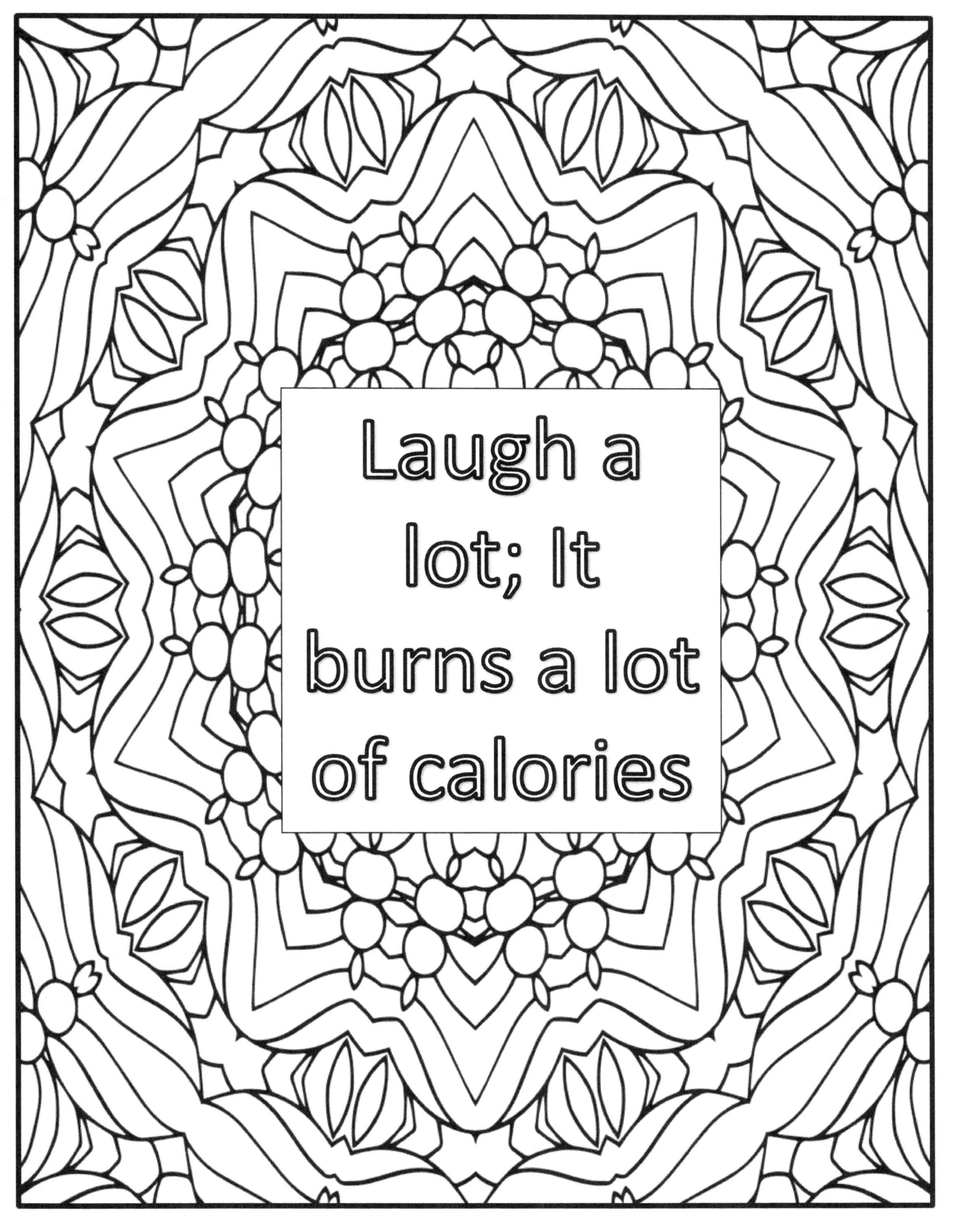

Laugh a lot; It burns a lot of calories

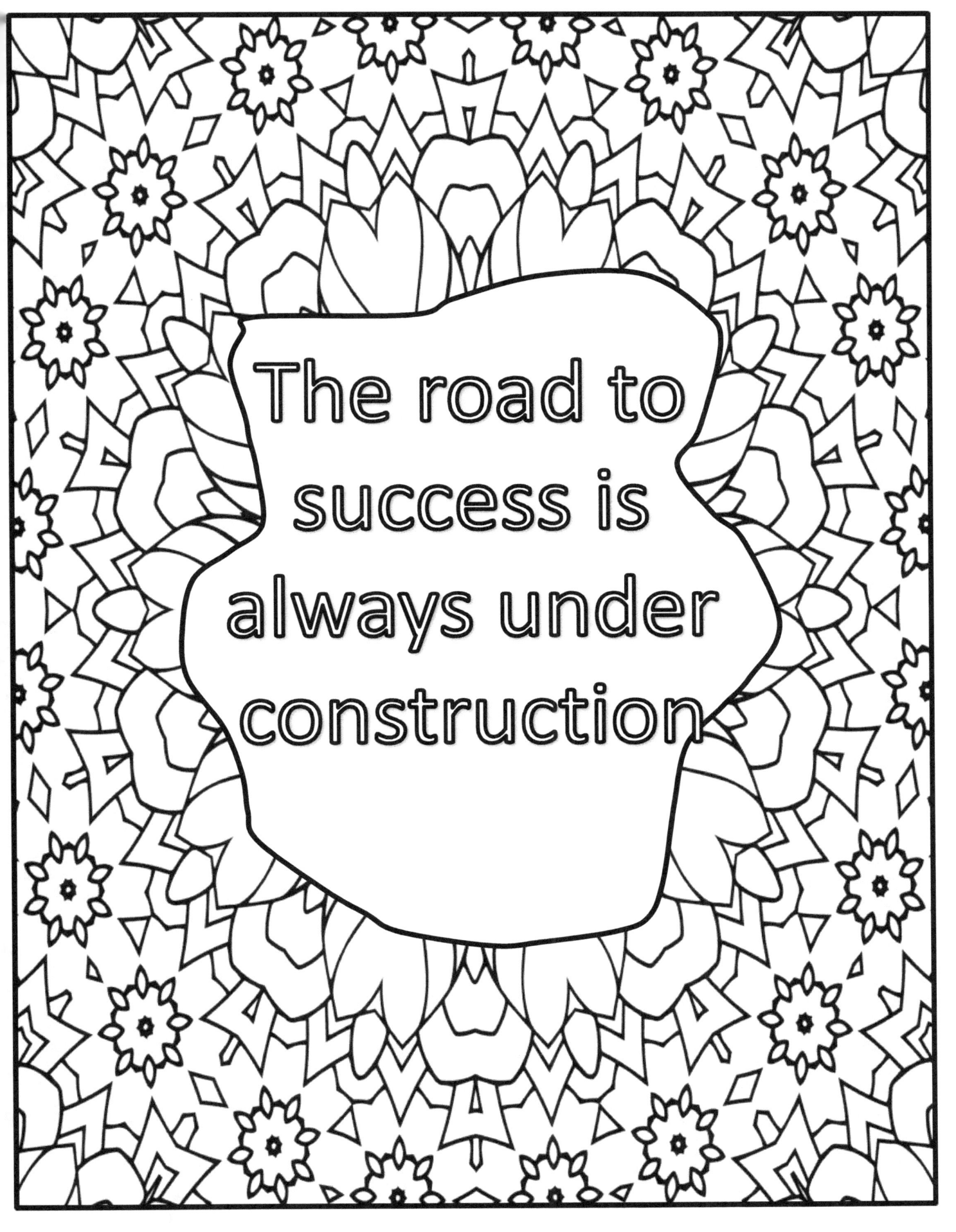

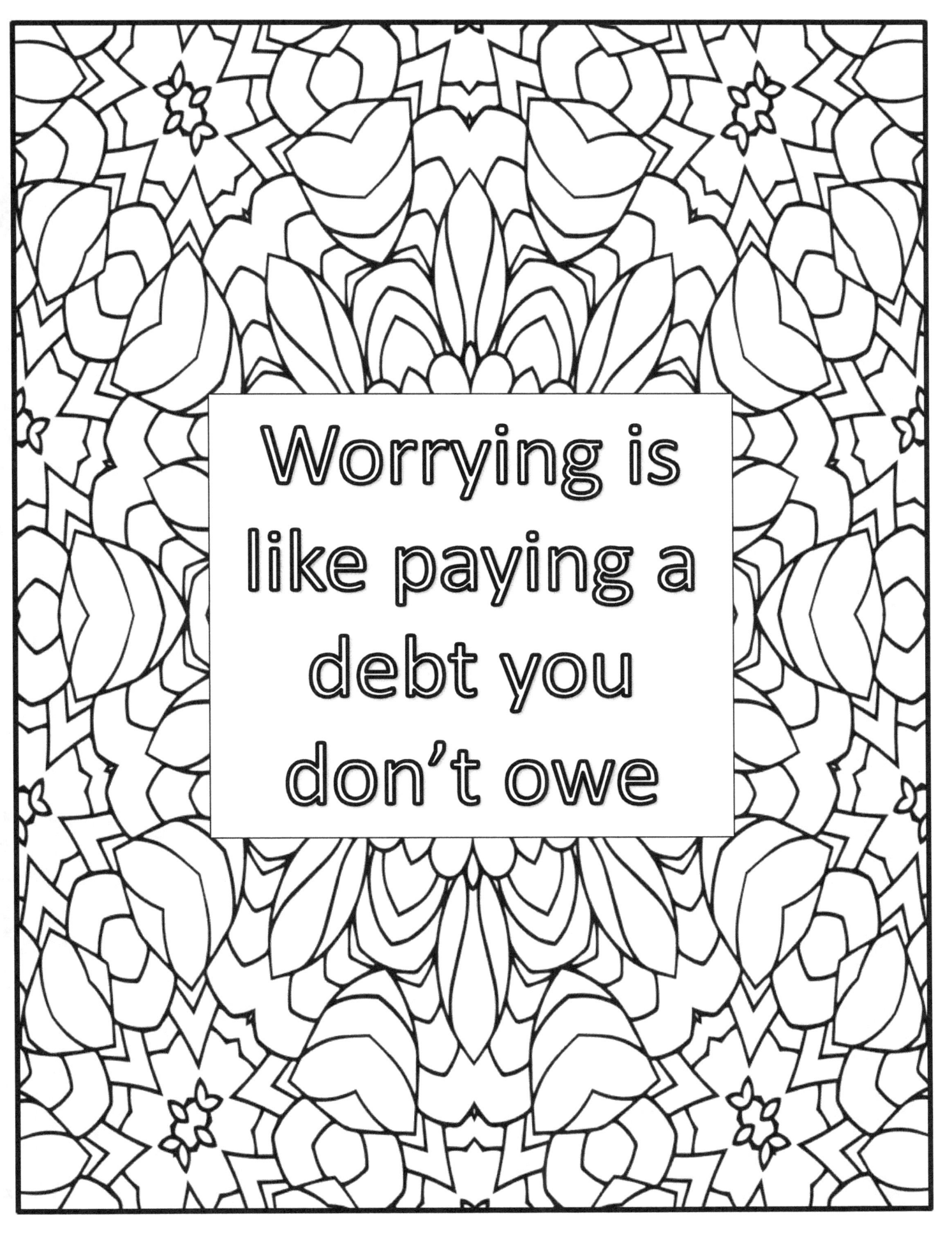

Worrying is like paying a debt you don't owe

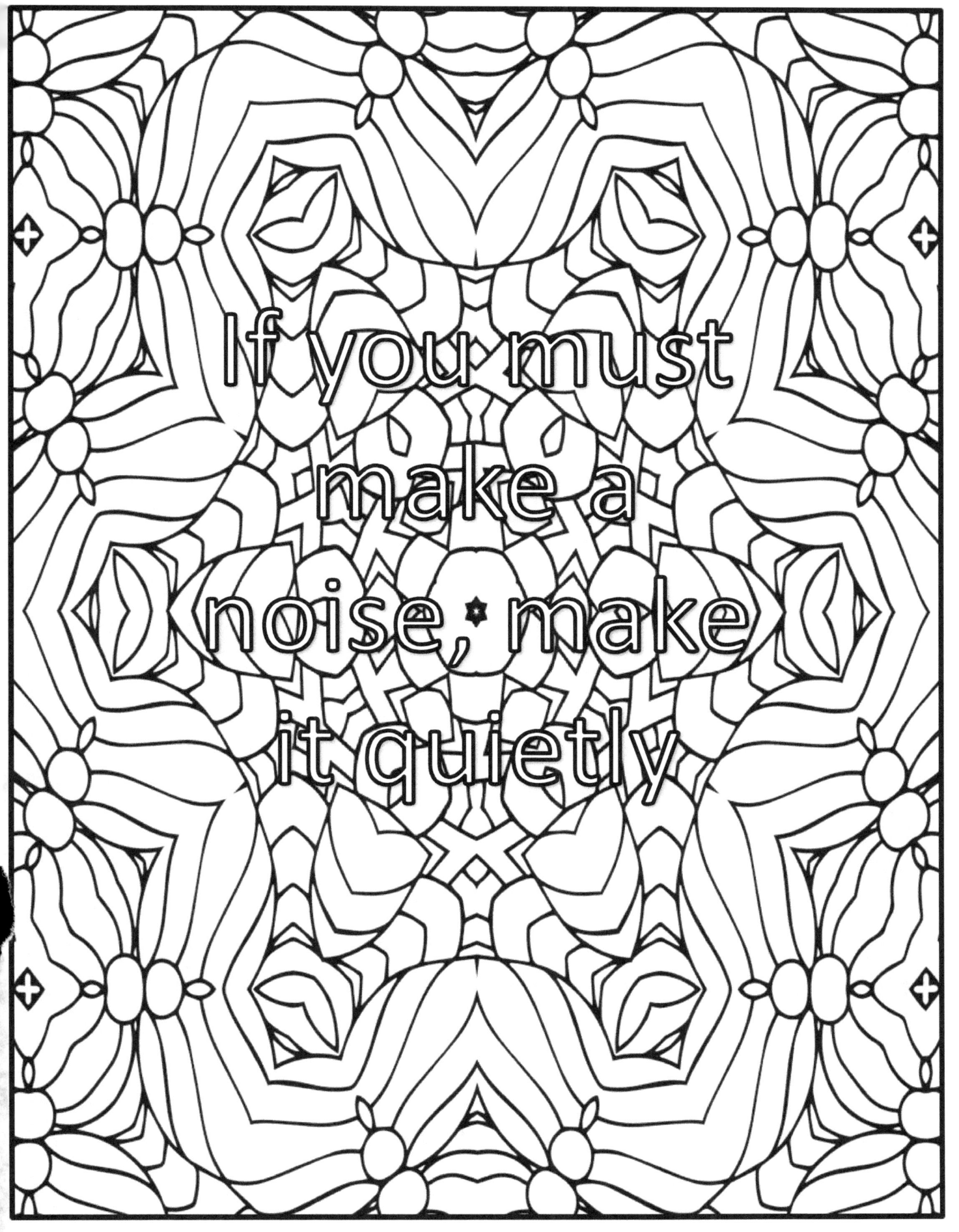

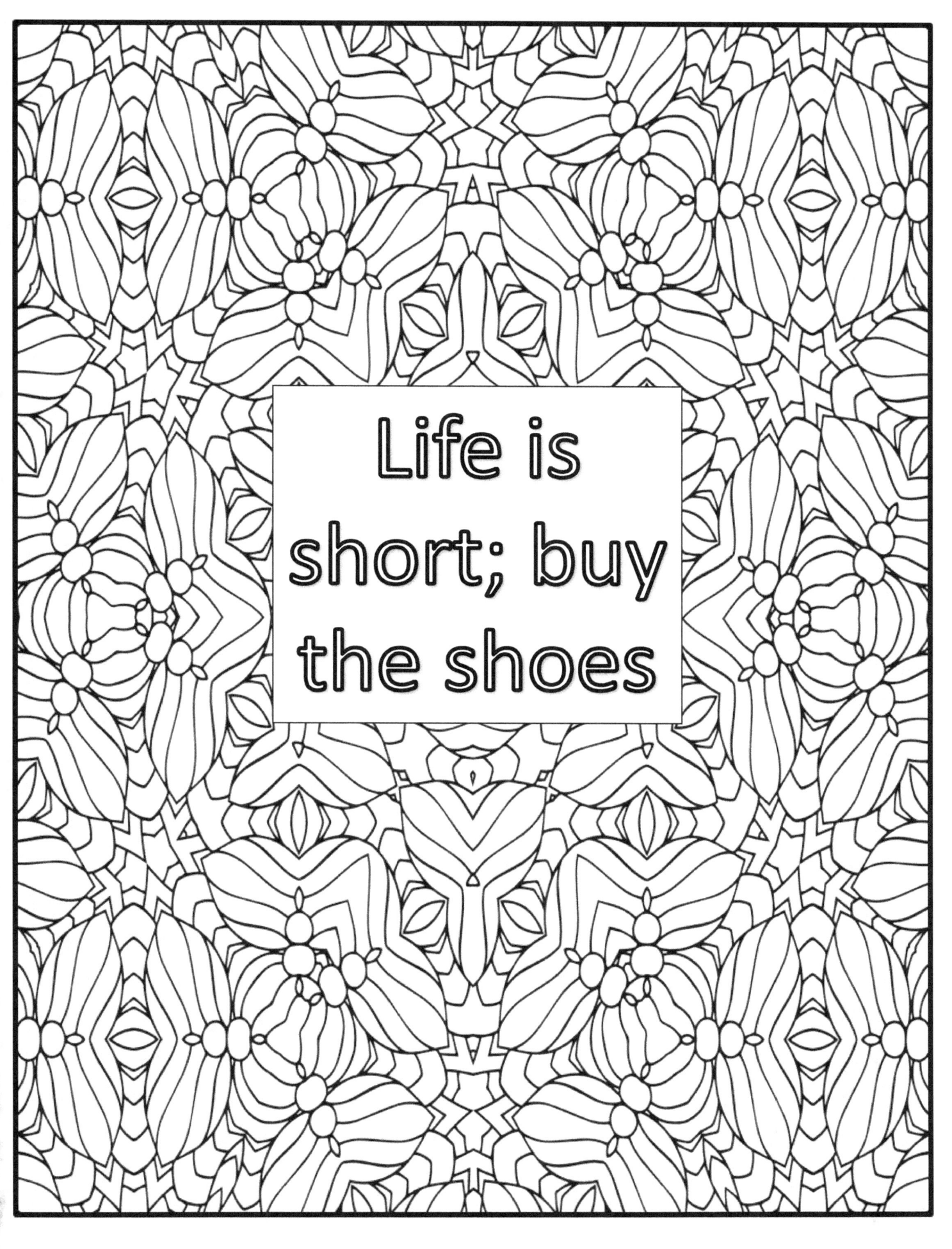